OVERVIEW

Overview

Learning about change helps you to realize that change is normal. It also helps you understand what's going on in your own organization and what steps you can take to prepare for changes that may affect your job.

Organizational change is change that affects the entire organization rather than a localized change.

When organizations make externally-driven changes, they are reacting to the immediate business circumstances they are in. However, making an internally-driven change is proactive and is often a result of innovative ideas.

Organizations strive to create stability, but they are forced to adapt to changing environments. The incremental tactical changes that organizations implement on a day to day basis are strategic adjustments. It's relatively easy to adapt to a strategic adjustment. A few small things change, but most people's work stays very much the same.

Sometimes, organizations have to change their ways of doing things more significantly with strategic reorientations that involve changes to strategies and new ways of working. When an organization experiences strategic reorientation, people often have to acquire new skills, and the nature of their work may change significantly.

Organizations that experience major change are going through transformational change. This is uncommon, but when it happens it represents an upheaval and a change in the goals, identity, or nature of an organization. Transformational change has a very strong impact on employees and can be difficult to handle.

Common reactions to high-impact organizational change are negative, instigative, passive-aggressive, neutral, and positive.

When organizational change occurs, each person may move through six stages of reaction – shock, denial, anger, passive acceptance, exploration, and challenge.

Your reactions to change affect the stages of reaction that you move through. The more positive your reaction, the quicker you move into the more positive stages of reaction.

Organizational change is inevitable, but can lead to feelings of fear and anxiety. It's important to be prepared because the ability to handle organizational change is highly valued by employers, and because the stress that accompanies change can have negative effects on your personal and professional life.

The characteristics of people who handle change effectively are the ability to acknowledge and share their feelings about the change, a willingness to take risks, an openness to the unknown, and having a good support system of family and friends.

Two kinds of skills needed to handle change effectively are self-management skills and stress management skills.

Self-management involves identifying and constructively addressing your emotional responses to change, while stress management involves knowing how to deal with anxiety, tension, and frustration.

The self-doubt, confusion, and despondency that often result from organizational change can rob a person of all motivation and enthusiasm. So it's important to stay self-motivated by believing in yourself, thinking positive thoughts about the future, having strong goals to focus on, and cultivating a motivating and supportive environment.

To accept the reality of change in your organization, it's helpful to gain perspective. When you recognize that change is not in your hands, it's easier to let go of personal preferences. To guide yourself toward acceptance, you can express your feelings, use ceremony to mark the change, and assess your current and future circumstances.

When you observe yourself resisting change, you can analyze yourself to understand more about why, how, who, and what you're resisting.

Learning from past experiences helps you to accept and adapt to change more effectively. This puts your present situation into a more long-term context and restores your balance. It also allows you to draw on your experience by using successful strategies from the past.

Reframing allows you to gain a more positive perspective on change. This strategy helps you to step back so you can notice the underlying attitude that colors your beliefs and values. You can then consciously adjust these and re-think the situation more positively.

You can reframe a negative attitude about change by focusing on potential practical and emotional benefits the change may bring.

Proactively capitalizing on organizational change enables you to regain a sense of control and to become more passionate about your work.

To do this, you need to reinvent yourself and disengage from unnecessary aspects of your former role.

You should also determine how you can realign your career goals to meet the new circumstances. A flexible career plan enables you to target opportunities and advance your career when your organization changes.

CHAPTER ONE
Understanding Organizational Change

Benefits of change

Major organizational change is often unpopular – particularly with those expected to implement it. This isn't surprising because, by definition, a period of change is an unsettling and uncertain time – a voyage into the unknown.

Consider Arlene who's initially suspicious of the change initiative in her organization.

"I think the way we've done things in my department until now has been just fine. It seems to me that all this talk of change is just causing a lot of fear and anxiety."

Luckily, Arlene has a good manager, Daniel, who realizes that for Arlene to deal with the reorganization, she first has to understand some of the basic principles of change.

He talks to her about why organizations change, the different types of change, and what organizations can do to make change easier to deal with.

By learning about organizational change, you learn that change is normal and you're better able to understand what's going on in your own organization. This helps you to take proactive steps to prepare for changes that may affect your job in the future.

See each benefit of learning about organizational change for more information about it.

Organizational change is normal

Change is a defining characteristic of the world. Without change, organizations will fall.

An organization exists within a certain context and needs to adapt to that context. Change keeps an organization going and helps to ensure it remains functional within a changing environment.

For example, some organizations incorporate policies to correct historical race and gender imbalances. Others might make changes in response to environmental concerns or new legislation. These types of changes are good and necessary.

Understand what's going on in your organization

Change brings a range of reactions and behaviors that can be predicted in some form.

Understanding these gives you a better sense of what's going on around you and this helps you to feel more in control.

For instance, a common response to change is to resist it when it seems threatening or confusing. When you bear this in mind, it's easier to deal with the resistance in yourself and your colleagues.

Prepare for changes that may affect your job

By knowing what to expect and by understanding what's going on in your organization, you can begin to proactively prepare for change in your job.

A clearer understanding of what's going on helps you to integrate change into how you work, enabling you to adapt more effectively.

For instance, if you know your company is going to start an internship program, you can begin to prepare yourself mentally for the extra stress that is part of having to work with relatively unskilled newcomers and plan ways to allocate responsibilities to them effectively.

Question

What are benefits of learning about organizational change?

Options:

1. You understand that change is normal and so becomes less threatening

2. You're better able to understand what's going on in your organization, which reduces stress

3. You're better able to be proactive when preparing for changes that may affect your job in the future

4. You understand how to restore calm to your colleagues

5. You understand your organization is unable to help you deal with the change

Answer:

Option 1: This is a correct option. By understanding that change is necessary for survival, it becomes less threatening and confusing.

Option 2: This option is correct. By understanding what's going on in your organization, you're less likely to feel stressed and confused.

Organizational Change

Option 3: This option is correct. When you're better able to understand the situation and what's likely to occur, you can take action that will help you to adapt and integrate the change into your job.

Option 4: This option is incorrect. Although sharing your understanding may help colleagues, conflict management and emotional intelligence is more likely to help you with this task.

Option 5: This option is incorrect. Organizations can take several actions to help employees deal with change more effectively.

Defining organizational change

You'll be exposed to many different types of change throughout your working life. Change that affects the entire organization in fundamental ways is known as organizational change. Change that is relatively minor and is limited to your immediate environment, such as who you work with on a team, is known as non-organizational change.

See the types of change for more information on how to distinguish between them.

Organizational change

Organizational change typically involves widespread change in operational, cultural, and procedural aspects of your work. This may include changes in the mission and vision of an organization, a merger, or layoffs.

It may also involve changes in how the company operates – for example, the restructuring of teams, the introduction of new technologies, and the implementation of new quality programs such as Six Sigma or Total Quality Management.

Non-organizational change

Where organizational change is substantial and organization wide, non-organizational change has a more local or minor impact.

This type of change is limited in its effect – for example painting the copy room a new color, changing the time of a weekly team meeting, hiring new employees, or reassigning others that you're used to working with.

Follow along as Arlene asks Daniel to explain the different types of change.

Arlene: I must admit, I'm still confused about the difference between organizational and non-organizational change. Suppose our company modifies the forms we fill out when a customer complains. Is that organizational change or not?

Daniel: That's a good question Arlene. You see, if the forms are updated on an ad hoc basis, that's change, but it's not really organizational change as such.

Daniel: On the other hand, suppose our customer relations manager realizes we need to develop processes that transform the customer feedback we collect into tangible operational improvements.

Daniel: He raises the issue in a meeting, and gets approval from upper management to design and implement a new company-wide process for acting on customer feedback. Now that's organizational change.

Arlene: OK. I think I get it now. For example, if you were to promote Tom and as a result he'd no longer work with us – even though his absence would seriously affect our team's productivity – your action wouldn't be defined as organizational change, right?

Daniel: Right, because it would affect the team only, not the organization as a whole.

Arlene: But if the Marketing Department decides that all employees have to start wearing uniforms every day to project the right image to our customers, that would be an organizational change.

Daniel: That's right. You've grasped the difference between the two types of change very well.

Question

Match each example to the type of change it represents. More than one example may match to a type.

Options:

A. Changing focus from product quality to customer service

B. Hiring a new engineer to work with your team on a project

C. Implementing a new quality management system

D. Redesigning the office floor layout at your branch

Targets:

1. Organizational change
2. Non-organizational change

Answer:

Organizational change is implemented across the whole organization, so it includes changes in mission from quality to service and the implementation of new management or quality systems.

Non-organizational change is local in its effect and so includes changes such as the hiring of an employee and changes in the layout of an office at a single branch.

Change triggers

You now have a better understanding of what organizational change is. But what causes these changes? How is change triggered in an organization? Generally, the triggers of organizational change are either internally driven or externally driven.

See each trigger type for more information about it.

Internally driven

Internally-driven organizational change is instigated to move toward or realize long-term objectives. This trigger involves changing the way the organization works to increase its long- and medium-term impact on external business circumstances. It may also be a result of original ideas within the organization.

Generally, internally-driven changes include inventions, innovations, and original process improvements to products, processes, or even worker compensation.

Externally driven

Externally-driven change occurs as a response or solution to immediate and external circumstances. Typically these changes are reactive and take a short-term view.

Examples of externally-driven change include responses to new legislation, bad publicity, or competition from rivals.

Cody works for a soft drink company. Follow along as he discusses change at his company. Try to identify which changes are internal and which are external.

My company actively seeks ideas for new products from all its employees.

It's always trying to keep one step ahead and recently developed a new system to automate a formerly manual process. And it did this without having to resort to layoffs!

It sourced corn that wasn't genetically modified in response to fears around safety issues.

It also changed processes to keep in line with new environmental regulations.

In Cody's company, product innovations and changing to an automated system are internally-driven changes, while the changes prompted by consumer concerns and environmental regulations are externally driven.

See each employee to discover further examples of internal and external triggers for change.

Emily

"Our customers demanded more automatic ordering procedures, so we decided to build a secure order form on the company's web site. Our site now offers a convenient, 24-hour service. This change was externally driven, because it was a response to feedback from our customers."

Gabriel

"My company had already switched to green processes, architecture, and materials before the environmental and building regulations began recommending them, so that change was internally driven. An externally-driven change that we've been through involved changing the way we record finances – this was in response to the Sarbanes Oxley Act."

Question

Match examples to their corresponding trigger types. More than one example may match to a type.

Options:

A. The company modified the manufacturing process in response to escalating costs of raw materials

B. An organization hired and trained new employees when demand for two of its products increased

C. To reduce costs in the long-term, the organization outsourced two of its internal processes

D. The organization diversified as a strategy for long-term gain

Targets:

1. Externally-driven change
2. Internally-driven change

Answer:

Changes in response to the escalating costs of raw materials or an increasing demand for products are externally-driven changes.

Internally-driven change includes outsourcing and diversification because these are long-term strategies for the organizations.

Three levels of change

Organizations strive to maintain stability. This means they constantly try to keep things the same. But, because organizations compete in a changing environment, change is inevitable. Usually, this change is gradual or evolutionary and only has a small to moderate effect on the organization and its employees.

An organization may encounter three categories of organizational change based on the intensity of change. The category with the least impact is strategic adjustments. The next category – strategic reorientation – is more intrusive. More rarely, an organization has to undergo a transformational change. This category of change is often risky and difficult.

See each change type for more information about it.

Strategic adjustments

Strategic adjustments are generally minor day-to-day changes in the way an organization does things. They are the results of an organization's attempts to remain effective and profitable and usually have immediate benefits. They are evidence that the organization is flexible enough to react to changing conditions in its environment.

Strategic reorientation

Strategic reorientation doesn't throw out current practices, but reforms those that already exist in a significant way. It's about modifying strategies and changing how these strategies are implemented.

Strategic reorientation doesn't occur frequently, but is essential for a healthy organization. Employees usually have to acquire new skills and some job descriptions may change.

Transformational change

Transformational change involves a fundamental shift in ways of working and thinking. It springs from a new organizational vision, a new business model, or a drastic change in the business environment. These changes have widespread effects on the company's products, systems, customers, and capabilities.

Strategic adjustments require little extra learning, so they're usually easy to accept and cause less stress for employees.

For example, the data fields on customer records may have changed or an organization may change to a less expensive supplier of raw materials.

With strategic reorientation, change is more invasive. It has a greater impact on employees than strategic adjustment, resulting in a higher degree of stress, increased insecurity, and resistance to the change.

For example, an organization might expand its market to a new country or call-center employees, who previously dealt with incoming inquiries, may now have to actively sell products to customers.

Another example is when employees have to move to new offices or job descriptions change to some extent.

Transformational change is quite rare and organizations only resort to this type of change to survive. Naturally, transformational change is difficult. It usually puts great strain on the organization's employees. As such, it requires more learning, loss of familiar routines, or even loss of familiar faces. For those reasons, this type of change is difficult to accept for employees and difficult to implement for managers.

An example of transformational change is the widespread automation of processes that were previously manual. Another common example is when one organization merges with another as a result of an acquisition.

Alternatively, the introduction of teamwork into an environment where people are used to working independently within a hierarchical structure is transformational change.

A company also undergoes transformation if it completely changes its product or service. For example, many large IT services companies started out as mainframe manufacturers that transformed themselves as technologies evolved.

Question

Match the descriptions of organizational change to the type of change they represent.

Options:

A. Minor and gradual tactical changes with immediate benefits

B. Modifications and augmentations of medium- to long-term strategies and their implementation

C. New organizational visions that generate radical, comprehensive changes

Targets:
1. Strategic adjustment
2. Strategic reorientation
3. Transformational change

Answer:

Strategic adjustments are minor changes in day to day strategies. They're usually gradual and require only a few new skills from employees.

Strategic reorientation is about modifying and augmenting strategies and adapting how these strategies are implemented. Strategic reorientation doesn't occur frequently and usually requires employees to learn new skills.

A new organizational vision or a drastic change in the business environment triggers transformational change. It occurs infrequently, and has significant repercussions for the organization.

Change types in action

Transformational change is the most difficult to deal with as an employee because it's so disruptive. However, each type of change requires a good attitude about change in general in order for an employee to thrive.

Follow along as Catherine and Frank discuss the changes they've experienced at the bank they work for.

Catherine: Since I've been with the bank, we've gone through some changes, but none have been disruptive. It's true that the forms have changed quite a lot because we record more information about each customer. But that's easy to get used to.

Catherine says confidently.

Frank: Yes, that kind of thing happens often, but it's pretty simple to keep up with.

Frank says confidently.

Catherine: Last year was hectic though. There was a new emphasis on customer relations. That was when we got all that training on interpersonal skills. Some people found it hard to get used to, but I enjoyed getting better at relating to customers.

Catherine says thoughtfully.

Frank: At that time, I worked at a bank that went through a merger. Employees were laid off and many branches were closed. Some resigned – they couldn't handle the pressure. I think that's one of the major reasons why I came to work here.

Frank frowns.

Changes to forms are strategic adjustments experienced as minor changes in Catherine and Frank's work routine. The change in approach to customer relations is strategic reorientation. It requires employees to adapt, learn new practices, and adjust their outlook. The merger at Frank's previous job represents transformational change, which he found very difficult to cope with.

Question

Match each example of change to the type of change it represents.

Options:

A. Call center employees are trained in a new sales method

B. Sales meetings are now scheduled twice a week instead of once a week

C. A clothing retailer establishes a new branch in another city

D. A vehicle manufacturing company uses new alloys to decrease costs of production

E. Two airline companies are merged into one

F. A charitable organization replaces its large pool of volunteers with paid employees

Targets:

1. Strategic adjustment
2. Strategic reorientation
3. Transformational change

Answer:

Strategic adjustments are minor changes in how organizations implement their strategies. Examples include changes to pitches used during customer sales calls and the frequency of regular meetings.

Strategic reorientations are significant changes in the strategies of an organization, such as establishing new branches or using new materials in production.

Transformational changes are major changes that transform organizations. They represent a change in goals and identity, and include situations such as mergers or a fundamental change in the organization's business model.

Gabriel, Arlene, and Daniel are discussing experiences of transformational change in organizations they've worked in. Select each individual to find out how that person dealt with transformational change.

Gabriel

"I went through transformation in our organization when our biggest competitor went under. Even though this was during a recession, the company knew it had to expand to fill the gap in the market. It was a huge opportunity – but very stressful. Lots of overtime.

I was given new responsibilities that I had no experience in and had to think on my feet. For a while I thought we weren't going to make it. But we did. Now the company is stronger than before and I've grown with it."

Arlene

"My company nearly went under. The whole system changed. New protocols, new legal compliance issues. It was a huge financial strain.

I know it had to happen, but it didn't work out so well for me. A lot of fingers were pointed. People felt very insecure about their jobs. And multiple investigations took place into how we had been working up until then. We had to account for everything we'd done.

Even though I wasn't actually blamed for anything, I still felt like I wanted to get out of there."

Daniel

"I experienced change when I was working for a small electronics retailer. Suddenly the market was flooded with cheap imports.

The company tried to adapt, but it couldn't. It was forced to close. The worst thing for me was going into work every day and not knowing what was going to happen or whether I still had a job. Since then, I've tried to ensure that organizations I work for are flexible and innovative.

I found the insecurity really hard to cope with. I think if innovation and expectation of change is part of a company's culture, it has a better chance when change comes."

Gabriel, Arlene, and Daniel all found transformational change difficult and frightening. However, they are proof that a positive attitude definitely helps an employee manage change more effectively.

Question

In the past year, what kind of change have you experienced in your organization?

Options:

1. Small shifts in how to do things
2. A change in procedure requiring new skills
3. A major upheaval

Answer:

Option 1: Small shifts in how to go about your work are indications that your organization has been making strategic adjustments as it tries to become more effective.

Option 2: If your work has changed focus somewhat, it may indicate that your organization was structurally reorienting itself to cope with new demands and pressures. These can sometimes be quite disruptive, but are generally manageable.

Option 3: If you and your colleagues have experienced a major upheaval at work, it may well be because your organization has been transforming itself. This can be a nerve-racking and demanding affair, in which the outcome is sometimes unclear.

Change reactions

How have you reacted to change in the past? Did you question those initiating the change, wondering whether they really understood what was needed? Did you recall past changes and assume that this one would be similar? These responses are common – when changes are initiated, people may recall past changes that were difficult or may question those who felt the change was necessary. These are key factors that make organizational change so hard to deal with.

Understanding the common reactions to change may help you recognize these tendencies in yourself. This helps you to be better prepared to take a healthy approach to change when it comes. It can also prepare you to help your coworkers deal with change.

Common reactions to organizational change include negative, instigative, passive-aggressive, neutral, and positive reactions.

See each reaction for more information on how to recognize it.

Negative

Employees with a negative reaction to change assume the change will be bad for the business, their colleagues, and themselves.

With a negative reaction, people are resentful of the change and may experience strong negative feelings such as frustration, anger, and annoyance. They feel that the change is unfair or they fear for the future.

Employees who react negatively are likely to complain – for example they'll say negative things such as "I think these new monthly deadlines are totally unworkable." They're also more likely to fail to contribute to discussions or to complete work.

Instigative

When employees react as instigators, they attempt to get others to oppose or resist the change with them. They spread feelings of mistrust and lower morale.

For example, they may try to get others worked up so that they oppose changes or to act in ways that impede the success of the change.

Passive-aggressive

A passive-aggressive response is also negative in nature but is less overt than open anger or attempts to instigate retaliation in others. It appears like cooperation on the surface, but people with this response are subtly sabotaging the process.

For example, the person may agree to change a process and then fail to carry it out in the new way.

Neutral

A neutral response is where someone decides to "go with the flow" or to wait and find out how the change pans out. Employees who experience neutral responses to change won't join in with the negative, change-resisting crowd, but neither will they support the change. They're more likely to be undecided about it.

"Let's see what happens" is a typical outlook that indicates this type of reaction.

Positive

The opposite of a negative reaction is a sincerely positive reaction. Some people react positively with curiosity and enthusiasm. They perceive the change as a challenge that motivates them to learn, grow, and succeed. They want to explore the issues associated with the change and want to proactively integrate the change.

Positive responses are apparent when people ask questions that show a positive desire to find out more – for example "So how long will it take to redesign the input forms for this?"

Another signal is when people want to address the challenge – for example "What's the best way to incorporate this?"

Question

Match common reactions to change with the corresponding examples of individuals exhibiting those reactions.

Options:

A. Negative
B. Instigative
C. Passive-aggressive
D. Neutral
E. Positive

Targets:

1. "I think this process will take too long and double the workload."

2. "The managers don't have any idea of how we work and are just priming us for layoffs."

3. "I told management I'd provide a list of potential new clients, but I haven't gotten around to doing it. I mean, what's the hurry?"

4. "I'm going to go with the flow and see what happens."

5. "I'm interested in how this might improve product quality."

Answer:

People who make pessimistic comments are assuming that the results of change will be bad and are responding negatively.

People who try to motivate others to resist change, for example by trying to get their colleagues to act against management, are playing the role of instigators against change.

People who say they're going to do things and then fail to follow through are often responding in a passive-aggressive way – sabotaging change without taking direct action against it.

When people suspend judgment and wait for what happens next, they're adopting a neutral attitude toward change.

Expressing interest in the positive outcomes of change is a sign of a positive reaction in an employee.

Stages of change reactions

You may have heard of the five stages of grief. Did you know a person may experience a similar set of reactions to drastic organizational change? Feelings toward change can develop over time within employees as they go through the six stages – shock, denial, anger, passive acceptance, exploration, and challenge.

Review each stage for more information about it.

Shock

In the shock stage, you feel numb – you aren't really taking in the idea that change is happening. You may find you need others to repeat themselves and you don't really feel anything either positive or negative about the change. In this stage, you need to take some time to address the reality of what's just occurred.

People in this stage may say things such as "I'm not sure how I feel about this, I need some time to think about it."

Denial

Once the shock wears off, you may find you refuse to accept the impact the change may have on you and your work.

People in the denial stage continue as though nothing has changed and may even say things such as "The restructuring won't affect my work."

Anger

Once the realization hits that the change will affect you, you may find you feel angry and want to resist the change or actively attack the change. You may find that you complain and question the value of the change.

People may say things such as "This change will ruin our productivity," or "The logistical implications are totally ridiculous."

Passive acceptance

Once you've realized the change will occur regardless of how you feel, you're likely to accept it and feel you may as well deal with it and get on with your work. Phrases such as "Let's just get on with it," are typical of the passive-acceptance phase.

Exploration

While in the exploration stage, you start to have an interest in the change and what it could mean for you. You begin to feel curious about how to implement the change and go forward with it.

Employees in this stage are likely to ask questions to find out more about the change and the processes for implementing the change. For example "How will we access the information we're going to need?"

Challenge

In the challenge stage, you become more enthusiastic and you start to believe in the value of the change. You

Organizational Change

begin to actually move forward in implementing the change and proactively try to integrate it into your working life.

In this stage people may say things like "This new and much closer relationship we're going to have with marketing is exactly what we need," or "I'll do everything I can to collaborate with others so that this sharing of information works."

Question

Sequence the order of the stages of reaction you typically go through in response to organizational change.

Options:

A. Shock
B. Denial
C. Anger
D. Passive acceptance
E. Exploration
F. Challenge

Answer:

Shock is ranked the first stage. Shock is the first stage of the response to significant organizational change. When confronted by change, you're in a state of disbelief.

Denial is ranked the second stage. Denial is the second stage of responding to significant organizational change. It's characterized by your refusal to admit the change will affect you.

Anger is ranked the third stage. Anger typically occurs after the denial stage. Here you start to question the value of the change and complain about it.

Passive acceptance is ranked the fourth stage. Passive acceptance is the fourth stage and generally occurs before the exploration stage. You start to realize that no matter how much you complain, the change is here to stay. You start to accept it, but haven't fully done so.

Exploration is ranked the fifth stage. The exploration stage is the second last stage and generally occurs after you've passively accepted the change.

Challenge is ranked the sixth stage. The final stage is the challenge phase, where you actively and enthusiastically embrace the change. You start to proactively integrate it into your daily work life.

Predicting responses

Individuals may not go through all the stages of reacting to change. The initial reaction to the change influences the future stages that someone will experience. The more positive your initial reaction to change is, the sooner you'll arrive at the place where you can feel enthusiastic about it and embrace the challenge.

When people are first confronted with change, they frequently react with shock, denial, or anger. At this early stage, change is often unexpected and experienced as a disruption. This may be unsettling and be seen as potentially threatening.

Once people have had time to come to terms with change a little better, they calm down and reach a point of passive acceptance. They aren't in the grips of strong emotion, but haven't reached the point of welcoming change or being proactive. So they feel neutral.

Once people have become neutral about change, it's possible for them to start understanding the implications of the changes they are experiencing. As they perceive new opportunities and begin to understand what's happening, they can start actively engaging with the change. This helps people to feel more empowered and they become more positive, investigating the situation with curiosity and renewed enthusiasm.

Emily used to work as a manager at a manufacturing company. When a larger soft drink company bought out the company, she was moved to the new head office. Follow along as she expresses her feelings about the changes.

When we first heard about the merger, I was really shocked. I thought our company was doing really well as it was, and I was afraid for the company and for my job. I couldn't believe it was happening and told myself it wouldn't really affect my work.

However, when I was moved to the new head office, I was really angry. The impact of the change and how it was going to affect me began to sink in. I became overwhelmed and kept thinking about how, after many years of hard work, I was being set up to fail.

Additionally, we were told to adopt the soft drink company's management strategy, which would cause a massive amount of work for me. It seemed counter-intuitive and unproductive. I decided to keep using our old processes, without saying anything.

In the end though, I realized if I wanted to keep my job, I'd better just get on with it and learn the new ways of doing things.

Emily's reaction is fairly typical. Her initial response was a negative one and she moved through shock, denial, and anger. In the anger stage, she reacted with angry thoughts and behaved in a passive- agressive manner as she silently resisted the change. She then moved into the passive-acceptance phase and her attitude became more neutral. If all goes well, she'll eventually move on through the positive stages.

Cody works for the soft drink company and has some experience with change because of the company's history of innovation. However, everyone at the company is quite tense, not knowing what to expect. Follow along as Cody discusses his reactions.

I was really surprised to hear about the merger and had to ask a couple of times what was really happening. I needed a day to get my head around what I was hearing.

Once the news sunk in, I decided to just go with it and observe what would happen and how it would work out.

Within a few days I became quite curious about the manufacturing company. I'd heard good things about it and wanted to find out what lay ahead for us. I was curious about its cross-departmental teams and tried to find out more about how they work.

I then tried to collaborate effectively with other departments, as the team structure seemed like it could really work well.

Cody was shocked by the news of the merger – a typical first response. His reaction was positive, though, as he'd heard good things about the manufacturing company. This helped him to skip denial and anger, and he moved directly to passive acceptance. From there he moved on to an even more positive mind-set as he entered the exploration and challenge stages.

See each employee to find out about the benefits and negative effects of Emily and Cody's responses to change.

Emily

Emily experienced a range of negative effects because of the way she dealt with the change. Her negative reaction increased her stress levels, which affected not only her work but had the potential to spill over into her personal life as well.

The way she spread her fears may also have affected her coworkers negatively, generally increasing their stress and lowering morale. Her pessimism blocked her from identifying potential opportunities for her organization and herself, and from responding creatively to the challenges.

Cody

Cody's response to the change provided several benefits for him personally, as well as for his manager and coworkers.

His enthusiasm and curiosity helped those around him to feel more confident and optimistic, and modeled a positive response. He was able to play a proactive role in the changes, investigating new opportunities and making the transition more likely to succeed.

His attitude enabled him to learn from the change, so he gained important insights, more confidence, and more experience. In fact, he found that the changes brought exciting new challenges and made working in his organization a lot more fun.

Cody's positive attitude and team spirit, as well as its positive effects, were noticed by his organization, so he became more respected and was able to advance his career.

From Emily and Cody's experiences, it is clear that your reactions can have negative and positive effects on your health, your home life, and your workplace.

The results of a negative reaction can cause much harm:
- it produces a feeling of anxiety and stress, which will in turn lead to decreased productivity,
- it leads to a drop in effectiveness, which your supervisors will notice, so you may miss out on advancement opportunities,
- it increases your coworkers' levels of stress, which contributes to low morale at work, and
- it impacts your home life as well if you become moody and tired.

A positive reaction enables you to feel more confident and optimistic about the future. Playing a proactive role in the changes allows you to learn from the change. You will be more open to a sense of excitement about the new challenges and to a sense of adventure and fun. Your supervisors will probably notice a positive team spirit, which will earn you a reputation as a respected and valued employee.

Case Study: Question 1 of 3

Gabriel's company has decided to reduce its workforce by 30% due to a serious downturn in the market. Gabriel will not be laid off himself, but will lose many of his coworkers. To make matters worse, Gabriel is asked to take on the work of one of his colleagues as well as his current workload.

On hearing the news, Gabriel says the extra duties won't affect him much. But then he speaks with his supervisor, expressing his distrust in the change. He also misses a deadline for handing in a report he had to complete for a colleague who was cut from the workforce. Although he isn't admitting it, he could have handed in this report on time.

Answer the questions in order.

Question:

How would you label Gabriel's initial reactions.

Options:

1. Passive-aggressive
2. Negative
3. Positive
4. Neutral
5. Instigative

Answer:

Option 1: This option is correct. Gabriel said the extra duties wouldn't affect him much, but he failed to follow through and missed a deadline he could have met. This implies that he is reacting in a passive-aggressive way.

Option 2: This option is correct. Gabriel purposefully missed his deadline and he spoke to his supervisor about his feeling of distrust in the new process, so he had a negative response to change.

Option 3: This option is incorrect. Gabriel made no positive comments about the change, nor did he rise to the occasion by meeting his deadline, so he hasn't reacted positively at all.

Option 4: This option is incorrect. Gabriel expressed distrust and purposefully missed a deadline, so he's not reacting neutrally to the change in his workload.

Option 5: This option is incorrect. Although Gabriel spoke to his supervisor about his mistrust in the process, he didn't try to get his colleagues to take action against it, so he didn't respond as an instigator to the changes.

Case Study: Question 2 of 3

Based on what he said and did about the changes in his company, what stage of reaction do you think Gabriel is currently at?

Options:

1. Anger
2. Denial
3. Shock
4. Passive acceptance
5. Exploration
6. Challenge

Answer:

Option 1: This is the correct option. Gabriel expressed mistrust in the changes at his company and failed to meet his deadline, so he's showing signs of anger.

Option 2: This option is incorrect. Although Gabriel said the changes wouldn't affect him much, he's acting passive-aggressively, which suggests anger rather than denial.

Option 3: This option is incorrect. Gabriel is acting out through his passive-aggressive behavior and he's expressing mistrust actively. So it's unlikely he's still in the shock phase.

Option 4: This option is incorrect. Gabriel said the changes wouldn't affect him, but then he purposefully missed his deadline – indicating he's in the anger stage and has not yet accepted the changes.

Option 5: This option is incorrect. Gabriel hasn't expressed any curiosity about the change in his company or what its implications are. He's still in the anger stage of reacting to change.

Option 6: This option is incorrect. Gabriel hasn't shown any enthusiasm or been proactive about the change in his company. He's still in the anger stage of reacting to change.

Case Study: Question 3 of 3

What results can Gabriel expect from his reactions in the coming days and weeks?

Options:

1. He'll feel stressed and anxious about his job
2. His supervisor may feel more pessimistic and mistrustful about the change after listening to him
3. If all goes well, he'll probably come to accept the changes, explore their implications, and eventually develop a more positive attitude
4. He'll be less effective at work
5. He'll act as a positive catalyst for change in the company 6. He'll be able to take full advantage of new opportunities

Answer:

Option 1: This option is correct. Because he's been given additional responsibilities and is experiencing anger, he's likely to feel insecure about his position within the company and hence more anxious and stressed.

Option 2: This option is correct. Gabriel's comments to his supervisor may influence her opinions and attitudes, so she may feel more pessimistic and mistrustful about the change.

Option 3: This option is correct. Gabriel is reacting in anger now, but, if all goes well, he'll probably move into later stages of acceptance, followed by exploration and rising to the challenge.

Option 4: This option is correct. Gabriel's feelings of anger and his passive aggression will make him less capable of a creative, problem-solving approach, so he'll be less effective at work until he feels more positive.

Option 5: This option is incorrect. While Gabriel's in the negative stages of reaction to change, he won't be able to act as a positive catalyst in his organization, because he's feeling unmotivated and stressed.

Option 6: This option is incorrect. Gabriel is resisting change and mistrusts the process, so he probably won't be very good at noticing and responding to potential opportunities.

CHAPTER TWO
Preparing for Organizational Change

Preparing for change

Have you ever been anxious or fearful of a change that was taking place in your life, even though you knew it was necessary? Consciously you might know that change often brings unexpected opportunities, but change can still make you feel uncomfortable – particularly when you have no control over it, or it's your job or workplace that's changing.

Organizational change can be due to mergers, technological progress, new thinking, or layoffs. Only one thing's for certain – no matter where it comes from, change is bound to happen.

So it's vital to be prepared for organizational change. If you embrace it, you won't be overwhelmed by the feelings of grief or anxiety that often accompany uncertainty.

That's why employers value employees who are change agents – people able to cope with and facilitate change in the workplace. Change agents can be counted on to take care of business and make sure everything runs smoothly during times of upheaval. They look to the future, are self-motivated, are passionate, and understand others.

See each characteristic of change agents to learn more about it.

Look to the future

Change agents recognize potential for positive change in their personal and professional lives, and strive to achieve that vision. Their actions have focus and purpose, and they stay motivated by the possibilities the future holds.

Are self-motivated

Because they're able to look to the future, change agents are able to motivate themselves to get through their day-to-day tasks for the sake of a goal. They're able to stay motivated even when those around them are struggling with the change and are becoming unproductive.

Are passionate

Change agents are passionate people and are therefore able to inspire passion in others. They're energetic and enthusiastic about both their visions and the inevitable changes in the workplace.

Understand others

Change has a big effect on people. Change agents understand this and are able to identify with and influence others around them. They persuade and encourage their colleagues to accept change and to share their passion.

Being a change agent isn't just preferable – it's essential. When you become inflexible in your routine or thought, you can't adapt to progress. And then you might find yourself left behind or even without a job.

Fear and anxiety are normal, natural responses to change. People worry about adapting to new rules, processes, or lifestyles. They may be afraid it'll be too difficult, that they'll fail or be too slow to adapt, or they simply fear not being in control.

But when you let fear and anxiety take over, these emotions can be unhealthy. Without managing them appropriately, their effects can damage your personal and professional life.

Stress caused by fear and anxiety can have several harmful physical and psychological effects – such as lethargy and listlessness, or a feeling of being overwhelmed.

See each side effect of stress to find out more about it.

Lethargy and listlessness

Fear and anxiety can cause you to feel lethargic and listless. You may feel that you don't have the confidence or energy to face the challenges of the day or even your everyday tasks. You might find yourself thinking defeatist thoughts like "How can I possibly do all this?" or "Now what?"

Feeling overwhelmed

When change – something new and unknown – overwhelms you at work, you may feel unable to cope with the pressures of work and, as a result, your productivity may suffer. When this happens, you may find yourself on a downward spiral because when you're unproductive you become even more stressed and filled with anxiety.

While you can't avoid change, you can control your reaction to it. The first step to counteracting the negative emotions that can accompany change is to develop the right attitude to it.

To do this, you need to embrace change. You can seek out challenges and try unexplored methods or avenues. Take note of your familiar routines and thought habits, and deliberately alter them. That way, you'll practice being more flexible.

Question

Why is it important to prepare for organizational change?

Options:

1. Employers highly value the ability to embrace change
2. You are able to deal with the harmful effects of stress
3. You know how to avoid or prevent difficult transitions
4. You're able to bury feelings of fear and anxiety

Answer:

Option 1: This is a correct option. Because change is inevitable in the workplace, your employer will value it if you're able to embrace and affect change.

Option 2: This option is correct. Stress can have harmful effects on your personal and professional life, but you can avoid these effects if you embrace organizational change.

Option 3: This is an incorrect option. Change and transitions are unavoidable facts of workplace life. By accepting this, you'll be able to avoid the harmful effects of the stress that accompanies change.

Option 4: This option is incorrect. Denying or burying your feelings is unhealthy. But by accepting and embracing change, you'll avoid the harmful effects of these emotions.

Sharing feelings

People who can handle change effectively are those who acknowledge their negative feelings, are willing to take risks, stay open to the unknown, and have a good support system of family and friends.

Change can bring with it a host of negative feelings – you might fear the transition or find it painful. But because change is inevitable, change agents know there's no use resisting or avoiding it – this will only make the adjustment more drawn out and painful in the long run.

Similarly, trying to bury your emotions won't make them go away. It's healthier to acknowledge how you feel about change – both to yourself and to those in your company who are responsible for the change.

Acknowledging and sharing your feelings can take place at all stages of the transition. You could convey to management how difficult you find the change or how powerless you feel. And you can communicate your wish to embrace the change as the first step to making it a reality.

Risks and the unknown

Tanya is a valued project manager at her company. She's intelligent and creative, and knows how to trust her gut feelings on projects for which there's little precedent or information. When her department is merged with another, she's expected to make decisions on projects she knows little about. But she rallies to the challenge and her superiors are so impressed that she's promoted.

Question

Do you think Tanya might have been fearful or anxious about the merger?

Options:

1. Yes
2. No

Answer:

A willingness to take risks and tackle challenges head-on doesn't mean you aren't afraid or anxious about those risks – it means you accept your fears and learn to live with them.

As people who are willing to take risks, change agents generally have the ability to handle organizational change. They know how to deal with the natural fear that comes from facing something with unknown outcomes.

Your comfort zone is shaped by fear – both rational and irrational. Risk-takers are able to acknowledge and accept their fears, and then take action anyway.

Change agents like Tanya know that taking risks opens you up to a range of possible benefits – both known and unknown. They overcome their fear because they know that the rewards might well be worth it.

Tanya is willing to take risks because she stays open to the unknown. She doesn't shy away from unfamiliar situations but looks forward to the exciting possibilities that might come her way as a result of them.

Being open to the unknown doesn't mean you have to take leaps into the dark. You can minimize the negative possible outcomes of a risk by gathering as much information as you can and making contingency plans.

Successful risk-takers know how to prepare for the unknown by setting goals and to keep them on track no matter what gets thrown their way. They interpret new challenges as a chance to learn, rather than something to be afraid of.

Todd is a designer for a sports vehicle manufacturer. In response to the rising cost of materials, the company needs to undergo some changes to its manufacturing process – which is likely to affect Todd's work in a number of unforeseen ways.

Todd prepares for the change by gathering as much information as he can about the new process and how it'll affect his day-to-day work.

Organizational Change

His contingency plan is to ask his manager if he can undergo some training if it turns out he struggles to adapt to the new process.

And he sees the change as a chance to develop his creativity and test his problem-solving skills. He knows that what he learns will help him advance professionally.

Often, people who resist organizational change are the very same people who complain that their jobs are boring or mundane. But change is never boring – it's exciting and refreshing, and requires you to think creatively. Change agents open themselves up to the new experiences that make life interesting.

By being open to the unknown, you meet new people, find new opportunities, learn new things, and grow in your personal and professional life.

But that's only possible if you're willing to move beyond your comfort zone – to take risks and stay open to the unknown. You trust that the future will hold good possibilities – not just the negative ones you fear.

A good support system

Faye has a large base of friends and family who she knows she can rely on to help her out no matter what happens. So when she hears that the company she works for is downsizing, she's not as worried as some of her coworkers. She knows that no matter what happens, she'll be able to weather whatever storm comes her way – even if she gets laid off.

One of the best ways to handle stress is to have a good support system of family and friends who you can rely on.

People who are most likely to handle organizational change know that they can turn to their support system for help if they need to. Their friends act as a kind of safety net – with their support, you feel more certain of finding a way to survive the stress of change.

Recognizing change agents
   Case Study
   Scenario:

You're a senior manager at an insurance company that's about to merge with another firm. Henry, Lilian, Joel, and Luther work in your department and have different ways of dealing with the impending change.

Henry

Henry is a popular guy both in the office and out. He has a large family and looks forward to spending time with them. He knows the merger will encroach on his free time and says he feels powerless to prevent it. For that reason, he's not thrilled about the merger. He'd prefer if things stayed the same.

Lilian

Lilian has a large family and three young children who rely on her as the sole breadwinner. So she says she's somewhat anxious about the merger and worries about whether she'll be able to keep her job. In principle, though, she has nothing against it and looks forward to the new colleagues she'll meet and tasks she'll have to perform. She thinks a change is as good as a rest.

Joel

Joel has been doing the same job in your company for years. He's refused a few chances for promotion in the past because he says he's happy where he is. When you invite his feedback about the merger, he doesn't want to talk about it. Joel is looking forward to meeting new people because he doesn't have many friends in the office at the moment.

Luther

Luther is a loner who doesn't have many friends and his family lives in another part of the country. He devotes his energy to the company by throwing himself into his work. He says he's not really worried about the merger, although he doesn't think it'll be of much value to anyone. He's ambitious and says he'd love the opportunity to take on more responsibility by managing the merging of the departments.

Question:

Which of your employees shows the characteristics of someone who'll be able to handle organizational change?

Options:

1. Lilian
2. Henry
3. Luther
4. Joel

Answer:

Option 1: This is the correct option. Lilian acknowledges and shares her anxiety about the change, is someone who's willing to take risks and who's open to the unknown, and has a good support system to help her through the change.

Option 2: This option is incorrect. Henry has a good support system but isn't open to the unknown future that the merger will bring. He's open about his anxiety, but doesn't look forward to the potential rewards of the change.

Option 3: This is an incorrect option. While he's willing to take risks, Luther isn't as positive about the merger as he could be. He also doesn't have a good support system to help him through the change.

Option 4: This option is incorrect. Joel doesn't have a good support system and isn't sharing the anxiety he must be feeling about the changes he faces. He's also unwilling to take risks.

Self-management

Change happens all the time – it's inevitable. So it's essential to be able to manage change effectively. Two skills are essential if you want to manage change: self-management and stress management skills.

Question

What do you think self-management entails?

Options:

1. Controlling your reactions to emotions
2. Suppressing negative emotions while giving positive ones free reign
3. Concealing negative emotions only

Answer:

Self-management doesn't involve suppressing or trying to conceal your emotions. Rather, it involves identifying and finding constructive outlets for emotions with the potential to have damaging effects.

In times of organizational upheaval, employers value those employees who are able to direct, assess, and manage themselves. People who have these sorts of self-managment skills take independent responsibility for their conduct, so they don't have to be guided through the change at a time when managers have enough on their plates.

Marsha and Jeffrey work in the same department of a large telecommunications company. When their boss falls ill and leaves the company, another manager who doesn't know the proper protocol steps in her place. The team is struggling to get by without her know-how.

Marsha and Jeffrey react to the change in different ways. Select each photo to find out how this particular employee reacts to the consequences of change.

Marsha

Marsha hates it when her routines are disrupted and can't stand feeling that she doesn't have a firm hold on proceedings. So she resents the new manager and often lashes out at him.

She finds her usual tasks stressful because she's not sure what she's supposed to be doing. She becomes ineffective and blames her lack of productivity on her new manager's lack of experience.

Jeffrey

Marsha's colleague, Jeffrey, has tried not to let the transition worry him too much. Although he's anxious for things to go smoothly, he simply gets on with it and what he's supposed to be doing as best he can.

He knows what's really worrying him is that he'll have to build a new relationship with the new manager and prove himself to be the capable, hard-working employee that he is. So he does his best to show he's able to make the transition from one manager to another smoothly.

xMarsha's inability to manage her own conduct makes her unproductive, so she appears unprofessional. But because Jeffrey is able to manage his own emotions and conduct, he's able to weather the change successfully.

Employees who are good self-managers are more likely to handle change effectively. Self-managers are able to identify their feelings and determine the underlying cause of them, so they address the problem directly.

See each characteristic to learn more about it.

Identify their feelings

First of all, self-managers know how to identify what they're feeling. They take note of the signals and so become aware of their own emotions.

For example, you might recognize the tightness in your chest as anxiety or the tension in your shoulders as anger – your own signals are unique to you. You can only deal with your emotions when you recognize and take note of them.

Determine the underlying cause

After you've identified your feelings, you determine what's causing them. You try to determine the underlying source of the emotion – not just the trigger that set you off this time.

For example, you might be feeling angry because your company has shifted its service offering as a way to adapt to changing market forces. Try to figure out why you are angry. Is it because you don't believe in the new mission? Or because you know the requirements of your job are going to change?

Address the problem directly

Organizational Change

Once you've identified your emotions and have determined their underlying causes, you can address the problem directly.

For example, if your initial reaction is anxiety that's based on assumptions about the implications of the change – or a lack of understanding of the reasons for the change – you need to gather more information about it from your managers. Then the root of your anxiety will be removed.

Stress management

Another quality that allows an employee to handle change effectively is the ability to manage stress. Self managers know how to recognize signs that they're frustrated, tense, or anxious. But they also know how to deal with that stress – they know how to relax.

For example, Julio knows he has a tendency to get frustrated with his work as a project manager when his organization implements new project management policies. When he feels himself getting tense, he goes for a stroll during his lunch break to calm down. Otherwise, he knows he risks snapping at his team.

Roberta has had a stressful day at work because she's struggling to get to grips with the new software she has to use. When she gets home, she listens to relaxing music to calm herself down and feels better afterwards.

Wendell's company has had to move offices and so work has been chaotic and stressful. But he feels better after spending time with his friends, who make him laugh. This eases the tension he feels after the experience.

You can handle stress in several ways. You could try to get your mind off whatever's worrying you by listening to music, watching a funny movie, or chatting with friends and family. Exercise is a good way to diffuse pent up aggression. Or – if you're angry – you could try meditating or spending time in a natural setting to lighten your negative feelings.

How you handle stress is up to you. You might simply need to take time out from the situation or make the effort to stay positive through the stressful situation.

People who are able to handle change know how to keep themselves focused and calm in times of stress. By managing your time, recognizing what sort of emotional reaction you're prone to, and staying open to change, you remain adaptable.

Change management

Nikki has worked as a graphic designer for a successful women's magazine for several years. The media group that owns the magazine has recently decided to update the look and feel of the publication. Nikki and her team have to learn new methods of doing their jobs and they're no longer sure what's expected of them. Deadlines that were always stressful are now even more so because last minute changes and requests abound.

Despite all this, Nikki has remained much more calm than the rest of the team. Follow along as Tyrone tries to discover her secret.

Tyrone: This "new look" thing is really getting on my nerves. Just look at these comments I received from head office! It's not my fault these designs look so awful. Nobody seems to know what we're supposed to do anymore.

Nikki: I know, it's been a really stressful time. But I guess we'll just have to weather it – magazines go through

Organizational Change

fashions just like everything else. At least we'll be able to keep up with our competition once things settle down.

Tyrone: Hmm. I guess that's a more positive way of looking at it, Nikki. How have you managed to stay so calm and collected through this whole thing? Everyone else is on the verge of a nervous breakdown – but you haven't broken a sweat!

Nikki: Well, I am under a lot of stress, just like everyone else. I just know how to manage my reactions to adversity and I know what to do to handle stress. Tell me, what are you really anxious about? I know you find these last minute changes frustrating, but is there more to it, Tyrone?

Tyrone: Well...I guess I used to feel I had it all under control, and now I don't. And I'm worried I won't live up to the new expectations. I mean, what would happen then? Will I be able to keep my job? Maybe that's what's really stressing me out.

Nikki: I think that's a normal reaction, I certainly worry about job security. The trick is to acknowledge how you feel and to get it out in the open. Often just talking about it can help. Once you've identified the cause of your anxiety, you can address it. Develop a back-up plan, maybe, in case things do go wrong. But you'll probably find things aren't as bad as they seem.

Tyrone: That's true. And anyway, I guess if I'm that worried about my job, the best thing I can do right now is get on with it, rather than throwing my hands up in despair.

Nikki: That's the spirit. It can be easier said than done, though. Stress can really get in the way of your productivity sometimes – and it's unhealthy. So you should try to find ways to relax. When I feel the frustration welling up, I close my eyes and count to ten, and imagine myself somewhere restful.

Tyrone: That sounds relaxing.

Nikki: And when that fails, when I have a really bad day, I get rid of some aggression in my kick boxing class after work!

Tyrone: Ha ha! That could work too. Maybe I should join you today. Thanks Nikki, just having a laugh about the situation has really lifted my mood.

Nikki teaches Tyrone some self-management skills. She helps Tyrone identify the cause of his anxiety so he recognizes the situation isn't as bad as he thought.

Nikki uses stress management techniques to help herself through the change. She tries to look on the bright side of the change by focusing on the benefits it will have. She takes steps to deal with stress by getting some exercise or taking a breather once in a while. She also manages to make light of the situation while talking to Tyrone, which makes them both feel better.

Question

Devin's manager of several years has just been fired. The CEO has appointed a new manager who's vowed to "turn the department around" and "get rid of inefficiency." Devin and his colleagues are anxious about how their jobs will be affected and whether they'll be able to cope with the new methods and a new boss.

Devin tries to stay positive throughout the transition. He focuses on the ways the change will be good for him and his career. He jokes about the situation with friends from work and tries to hide his anxiety so as not to make his colleagues feel worse. Devin also thinks about his old

Organizational Change

boss a lot, wondering what he could have done to help him keep his job.

In what ways is Devin effectively handling the change?

Options:

1. He's trying to find humor in the situation
2. He's trying to look at the situation from a different perspective
3. He's spending time thinking about events leading to the change
4. He's covering up his anxiety

Answer:

Option 1: This is a correct option. Devin is right to try to find humor in the situation and to use the opportunity to develop his relationships with his colleagues.

Option 2: This option is correct. It probably won't be as bad as Devin thinks it will. He's right to try and look at the change in a new light and recognize the bright side of the situation.

Option 3: This is an incorrect option. Devin shouldn't waste his energy obsessing about past events he can't change and probably had nothing to do with.

Option 4: This option is incorrect. Devin should be open and honest about how he feels about the situation rather than trying to conceal his emotions, as talking about what he feels would be therapeutic.

Motivation robbers

It's important to have the right mindset when you face organizational change. Good communication, self-management, and stress management skills are all useful for handling change. But there's another essential skill – self-motivation.

The people who achieve their goals are those who have self-motivation – those who keep moving forward, growing, producing, and developing.

There's a big difference between thinking about something you'd like to do and actually doing it. That difference is self-motivation: an internal, self-powered driving force that allows you to overcome your doubts and fears. It's worth cultivating because it's the bridge that connects your dreams to your reality.

To find out how self-motivated you are, ask yourself a few questions:

- Am I motivated by fear of punishment or a sense of duty? Or by my personal goals?

Organizational Change

- When I drag my feet, is it because I'm indifferent, afraid, or feel incapable?
- Do I rely on other people or deadlines to make me work?
- When I meet an obstacle, do I get frustrated and give up? Or do I push on no matter what?

Everyone – even the most positive person – will struggle to stay motivated when faced with significant organizational change. You can fall prey to several mindsets that impair your ability to stay positive and motivated – at least temporarily. These include dwelling on doubts and fears, confusion, and hopelessness.

See each mind trap for more information about it.

Dwelling

Organizational change can prompt you to dwell on your doubts and fears. Your feelings of uncertainty, inadequacy, or lack of control can lead you to dwell on past failures or hardships that come back to haunt you. Thoughts like "Why me?" "Why now?" or "Why this?" can crowd in and paralyze you if you don't make an effort to replace them with more positive thoughts.

Confusion

When you don't have personal goals to focus on and motivate your actions, the uncertainty that accompanies organizational change can leave you floundering and confused. You can be plagued by thoughts like "What am I supposed to do?" or "What happens now?"

Hopelessness

Setbacks can have you believing you're incapable of getting back on your feet. A feeling of despondency and hopelessness can set in where you stop believing in yourself and your ability to succeed. Instead of thinking

"This one little thing won't stop me!" you think "I don't know why I even bother" "I just don't have the energy" or "It's no use; life's just too hard."

Question

Which mindsets rob people of self-motivation?

Options:

1. The perception that everything is out of control
2. Feeling lost and bewildered
3. The sense that making any effort is pointless
4. The idea that change cannot be avoided
5. Feeling that you could be doing more to achieve a goal

Answer:

Option 1: This is a correct option. Feeling helpless in the face of change you can't control can cause you to dwell on negative thoughts and make you despondent.

Option 2: This option is correct. Confusion can leave you without direction. Without clear goals in mind, you might struggle to motivate yourself.

Option 3: This is a correct option. Organizational change can leave you with a feeling of hopelessness that stops you finding the will to continue.

Option 4: This option is incorrect. Accepting that change is inevitable can be the first step to accepting it and moving on, and could even be seen in a positive light.

Option 5: This is an incorrect option. If you think you could be doing more to achieve a clear goal you have, this might prompt you to take action to achieve that goal.

Believe in yourself

When you face organizational change, several elements of self-motivation are important if you want to handle the change effectively. You should believe in yourself, think positive thoughts about the future, have strong, clear goals in mind, and ensure you're in a motivating environment.

The first, and arguably most important, aspect of self-motivation is believing in yourself. To do this, you need self-confidence and self-efficacy.

See each component of believing in yourself for more information about it.

Self-confidence

Self-confidence is a faith in your own potential that gives you the momentum you need to act and succeed. It begins with recognizing your strengths and all the things you've already achieved – and which skills you can build on. This encourages you to continue building on your achievements by creating new goals and believing you can achieve them. Once you do, you're inspired to do even more.

Self-confidence is self-perpetuating – it gives you the strength to keep going despite setbacks and it also inspires confidence in others. It allows you to think "I won't let this stop me!" rather than "I knew I wouldn't be able to do it."

Self-efficacy

Self-confidence is a general belief that you're capable, have potential, and will succeed. Self- efficacy is a more specific belief in your strengths to complete a particular task.

So if you have a high self-efficacy, you're more likely to set your sights higher and set more difficult goals for yourself. You'll have faith in your ability to achieve those goals and setbacks won't put you off. If you have a low self-efficacy, on the other hand, you'll be less likely to even try.

While believing in yourself is key to a happy and successful life, it's also important to strike a balance between self-confidence and overconfidence. By keeping yourself grounded and realistic, you avoid overstretching yourself or taking on more than you can manage.

Question

Due to organizational changes that have recently taken place, your boss has asked you to present all of the department's project proposals to the organization's board of directors. By doing so, she demonstrates her faith in your abilities.

Which of your characteristics show her you're able to handle it?

Options:

1. You often challenge yourself with difficult tasks

2. You reassure yourself by taking on easy tasks to build your confidence

3. You often take on big tasks you don't have the skills to accomplish

Answer:

Option 1: This is the correct option. This shows you have good self-confidence and self-efficacy because you have faith in your ability to achieve success in a new or difficult area.

Option 2: This option is incorrect. By not setting your sights high, you show you don't believe in your own ability to achieve success in a new area. Without this sort of self-confidence, you probably wouldn't do well at the meeting.

Option 3: This is an incorrect option. This demonstrates overconfidence, which can lead you to underprepare and overestimate your ability to perform. Believing in yourself means having realistic goals and working hard to achieve them.

Positive thinking

An aspect of self-motivation that's closely linked to believing in yourself is thinking positive thoughts – particularly about the future and what you're capable of achieving. If you expect to fail, it can become a self-fulfilling prophecy – especially when you have to work hard to achieve your goal. Having a positive view of the situation allows you to bounce back from mistakes and obstacles.

Question

When your manager asks to speak to you, do you immediately assume he wants to give you negative feedback?

Options:
1. Often
2. Sometimes
3. Rarely

Answer:

Organizational Change

Option 1: You're probably in the habit of thinking everything is your fault and that if your projects are successful, it's either due to other people's skills or mere luck. This kind of negative thinking can jeopardize your endeavors.

Option 2: If you react this way occasionally, you usually have a good, positive outlook on life but sometimes take things personally or assume the worst. You should try to replace those rogue negative thoughts with positive ones before they become a habit.

Option 3: If you're unlikely to think this, you're a very positive person with a happy, optimistic view on life and have faith in your ability to achieve your goals. You're probably successful in your endeavors because you don't let setbacks get to you.

You can do several things to become a more positive thinker. The first step is to become aware of your thoughts. You take note when you have a pessimistic thought – and interpret it as such.

For example, Samantha is annoyed about the widespread technology upgrades at her company, which are putting her projects behind schedule. Whenever she dwells on it, she gets despondent about how much work she's got and can't find the energy to continue.

But she starts to recognize the beginnings of the spiral and stops her negative thoughts in their tracks, so she can get on with her work.

When you do spot a negative thought, challenge it with a positive one by deliberately replacing it with a more optimistic view of the situation.

It helps to imagine what it would be like to achieve your goals. You create a vivid mental picture of that possibility and focus on it when you feel yourself sliding into negative thought patterns.

To focus on your goals, you develop statements about what you want to achieve and repeat them to yourself daily.

Practice makes perfect – so repeat the actions that encourage positive thought daily, until it comes naturally.

Question

Wendy works for a company that's busy relocating to new premises on the other side of town. Not only is everything in chaos at the moment, which makes it more difficult for Wendy to give good service to her clients, but the new location adds an hour to her daily commute.

Which attitudes will help Wendy weather the transition?

Options:

1. Staying upbeat about the advantages of the new premises

2. Taking note when she finds herself getting frustrated, and instead telling herself it'll work out

3. Taking note when she feels upset and telling herself to snap out of it

4. Being realistic and accepting that work will be more stressful from now on

Answer:

Option 1: This option is correct. Wendy will find it easier to handle the change if she deliberately thinks optimistic thoughts about the situation and focuses on the positive aspects of the change.

Option 2: This is a correct option. Wendy should recognize her negative thoughts for what they are and challenge them with more positive thoughts.

Option 3: This option is incorrect. While Wendy should take note of her negative thought patterns, she should try to replace them with positive thoughts rather than admonish herself.

Option 4: This is an incorrect option. Wendy shouldn't focus on the negative aspects of the transition but should try to replace her negative thoughts with more positive ones to help her through the stressful period.

Strong goals

Motivation needs to be directed at something. So to successfully motivate yourself, you need a strong set of clear, achievable goals to work toward and give you the direction you need. Goals motivate you because they're a kind of promise to yourself.

Goals can help you stay focused and motivated during times of organizational change, when you might feel despondent or distracted, and become unproductive. Developing strong career goals can help you reframe the change so you're encouraged to continue for your own reasons.

Goals help prioritize your time, and increase your self-confidence as you continue to achieve them. The best goals are specific and measurable, and are small or regular enough for you to track your own progress toward your larger objective.

The best goals aim to modify your behavior rather than achieve an outcome. For example, you might decide to enroll in a personal development course at your local college before the end of the season.

Or you could choose to become an active member of a career-focused extra-curricular group.

You might decide to identify and discuss with your manager two knowledge areas you'd like more experience in or skills-development programs you'd like to take.

Goals should also be sufficiently complex and challenging to be interesting, but not too difficult to achieve.

They should also contribute to a larger objective you have in mind – for example to develop your career or make yourself more visible at work. Goals are the milestones that let you monitor your progress.

Question

Tamryn works for a small daily newspaper that's just been bought out by a multinational media corporation. Her tasks and work processes are likely to change drastically in the near future.

What will help her stay focused during this uncertain time?

Options:

1. She's doing a journalism course in her spare time
2. She's suggested to her editor that the team does a short training course to develop their news writing skills
3. She tells herself she'd like to be a good writer
4. She tends to stick to the same kinds of articles

Answer:

Option 1: This is a correct option. This shows that Tamryn has strong, specific personal goals that she's working to achieve.

Option 2: This option is correct. Tamryn is clearly ready for a challenge and will see the new assignment as a chance to work toward her specific goal of developing her news writing skills.

Option 3: This is an incorrect option. This objective is vague and unfocused – Tamryn needs more specific goals to track her progress towards it, as she might not recognize the change as an opportunity to realize her ambition.

Option 4: This option is incorrect. This shows Tamryn doesn't challenge herself with small goals and tasks. Without these self-motivating goals she'd probably struggle to handle change.

Your environment

It's important to have a motivating and supportive environment to keep you self-confident, to remind you of your goals, and to keep your thoughts positive. The first three elements of being self-motivated are internal. A positive environment is the external force that supports these other, internal approaches.

You can take very specific steps to ensure your environment is as supportive as possible. For example, you could seek out supportive coworkers, search for teamwork opportunities, and try to get interesting assignments at work.

See each example of a supportive environment for more details about it.

Supportive coworkers

You can build relationships with people who are likely to be positive and encourage you to attain your goals. If you ask them to hold you accountable, you'll be more likely to focus on the task at hand.

Teamwork opportunities

Working with a team makes you accountable to others. If you also seek out fellow positive thinkers and change agents to work with, you'll be more inspired to work harder to attain your goal.

Interesting assignments

You can ask your boss for interesting assignments – seeking out challenges will keep you motivated and enthusiastic about your job in spite of the uncertain environment organizational change can create. You can also ask your boss for targets and objectives to keep you focused and help you measure your progress.

Question

Because of low circulation, the magazine Brian works for is about to stop printing hard copies of issues and will publish them online instead. As part of the switch, employees now telecommute. But Brian's worried he won't be able to perform as well outside of his office and away from his colleagues.

What can he do to make sure he stays motivated when he starts working from home?

Options:

1. Stay in touch with colleagues who'll check up on his progress

2. Ask his boss for challenging assignments

3. Work exclusively on easy, routine assignments

4. Regularly e-mail his colleagues for updates on office politics

Answer:

Option 1: This is a correct option. Brian can reach out and ask positive, supportive people to encourage him and hold him accountable for meeting his targets.

Option 2: This option is correct. By getting more interesting assignments, Brian can keep himself motivated and ensure his enthusiasm doesn't wane.

Option 3: This is an incorrect option. Brian should challenge himself with more interesting assignments so he doesn't get bored and demotivated with his job.

Option 4: This option is incorrect. While it's probably a good idea to stay in contact with his colleagues, he should do it so they hold him accountable for doing his assignments.

Case Study: Question 1 of 4
Scenario:
You work for an architectural firm that designs buildings for large institutions. Strict new work safety laws have recently been passed which require you to rethink your designs, often at extra cost to your clients. Your clients are often unhappy about this, as are your colleagues – everyone's struggling to meet client specifications without violating the new laws.

Answer the questions in any order.

Question:
Which attitudes show that you have faith in your abilities as an architect?

Options:
1. When you meet with clients, you speak clearly and hold your head high
2. You use your mistakes as a way to learn
3. You avoid raising difficulties
4. You trust that there won't be any setbacks or disappointments

Answer:

Option 1: This is a correct option. You should believe in yourself and stay confident, self-efficacious, and self-assured.

Option 2: This option is correct. You should remain self-assured and believe in yourself enough to bounce back from obstacles rather than let yourself get discouraged by them.

Option 3: This is an incorrect option. You should believe in your own self-efficacy and have faith in your capabilities.

Option 4: This option is incorrect. You should have faith that you'll be all right no matter what happens, but accept that mistakes and setbacks are a part of life, and use them as a chance to grow.

Case Study: Question 2 of 4

What shows you believe your career will develop anyway?

Options:

1. You refuse to think about the possibility of failure
2. You have a mental picture of creating buildings that will satisfy clients and building inspectors alike
3. You develop a mental picture of what it would be like to fail to help you avoid that outcome
4. You list all the possible setbacks of applying the new requirements

Answer:

Option 1: This is a correct option. When you start thinking negatively, deliberately change your perspective of the situation and try to see it in a more positive light to renew your enthusiasm.

Option 2: This option is correct. You can develop a vivid mental picture of what it would be like to succeed, and focus on that image when your thoughts slide toward negativity.

Option 3: This option is incorrect. Thinking about failure will probably demotivate you. You should create a vivid mental picture of your success to keep you focus and encouraged.

Option 4: This is an incorrect option. If you dwell on all the ways you could fail, you run the risk of getting discouraged and demotivated. Rather think positive thoughts about the future.

Case Study: Question 3 of 4

What can you do to give yourself direction and keep you on the right track?

Options:

1. Take a few e-learning courses to improve your knowledge of the new laws

2. Focus on developing those skills which you need to navigate conflicting demands from clients and the laws

3. Develop a five-year plan to set a target for the number of buildings you want to design

4. Aim to be a successful businessman

Answer:

Option 1: This is a correct option. You've set yourself a concrete goal which you can track your progress towards – a goal which focuses on your behavior rather than an outcome.

Option 2: This option is correct. You've identified the skills you need to develop to achieve an objective, and set yourself a measurable, attainable goal.

Option 3: This option is incorrect. This goal is a bit too specific and is outcomes-based rather than behavior-based. Rather aim for goals you know you can achieve.

Option 4: This is an incorrect option. This is a vague, ambiguous objective rather than a concrete goal with measurable results. You should aim for something more specific and immediately achievable.

Case Study: Question 4 of 4

What should you do to create a space which encourages you to pursue your goals?

Options:

1. Seek projects where you need to collaborate with your colleagues
2. Seek out people who will be supportive of your ambitions
3. Take on projects which are familiar and routine
4. Seek out reserved people who are realistic about how often your projects will fail

Answer:

Option 1: This is a correct option. Working within a team of positive and supportive coworkers will help hold you accountable.

Option 2: This option is correct. You should build relationships with people you encourage you to achieve the goals you set for yourself and hold you accountable.

Option 3: This option is incorrect. Familiar or routine tasks might make you bored and demotivate you. Interesting and challenging tasks will keep you moving forward.

Option 4: This is an incorrect option. You should seek out positive people who will encourage you to believe in yourself and your potential.

CHAPTER THREE
Embracing Organizational Change

Gaining perspective

Starting a new job, moving to an unfamiliar place, or dealing with the death of a loved one are just some examples of events that most people will experience at least once in their lifetime. Each event is associated with major change. So when you start a new job, you can't expect the company to be exactly the same as your previous job. You need to be able to accept that things will be different and that you have to do things differently.

Strategies for accepting change

People often resist difficult changes, making them reluctant to try out new experiences. Feelings such as sadness, loss, anger, anxiety, and helplessness are common.

It's helpful to gain perspective by viewing the situation in a broader context. Through self-analysis, you can address the root causes of negative reactions such as grief, fear or anger.

Organizational Change

One way to put things into perspective is to adapt strategies that you successfully used to deal with change in the past. This helps you to draw on previous experiences of change and gives insight into what to expect this time.

So you accept change and overcome resistance to it by gaining perspective, analyzing yourself, and learning from past experiences.

To get a better perspective on change, you need to understand that often you can't prevent change from happening. So instead of resisting change, you should try to make the most out of what's ahead of you. This outlook helps you to admit the reality of change as a part of your life, bringing a measure of peace and tranquility to the experience.

Another key to a more accepting perspective is to realize that change happens whether you resist it or embrace it. You can let go, stop fighting, and accept the situation as it is.

One important indicator that you're gaining a healthy perspective is the ability to talk about the change with your emotions in check.

Follow along as three friends discuss the changes that took place at their respective companies.

Angela: Our company relocated recently. I used to have my own office looking out onto a beautiful lake. I now sit in a cubicle and get really depressed whenever I remember what I've lost.

Angela looks downhearted.

Bruce: Where I work we get new protocols we have to follow every week. I dread checking my inbox because I know I'm going to have to implement some pointless new rule.

Bruce looks angry.

Eugene: You have to come to terms with the change your companies have introduced. When my company downsized last year, I realized quickly I couldn't fight it. Instead, I grew from the experience and am now looking forward to the challenges.

Eugene looks optimistic.

Question

Which statements in the dialog do you think show an accepting perspective towards change?

Options:

1. "You have to come to terms with the change..."
2. "...I realized quickly I couldn't fight it."
3. "...I grew from the experience..."
4. "...I'm now looking forward to the challenges."
5. "I...get really depressed whenever I remember what I've lost."
6. "...I'm going to have to implement some pointless new rule."

Answer:

Option 1: This option is correct. Eugene is showing an accepting perspective toward organizational change. He's had time to process his initial resistance and anxiety, and has come to terms with his experiences.

Option 2: This option is correct. Realizing he shouldn't waste his energy on fighting the change helped Eugene make peace with his new situation.

Option 3: This option is correct. Eugene has assessed his experience in comparison to the past and has noticed the advantages the change brings him.

Option 4: This option is correct. Eugene's looking to the future in a constructive way, giving him the right perspective to make the most of opportunities that the change brings him.

Option 5: This option is incorrect. Angela's still mourning what she's lost, which indicates she's resisting the change. But by expressing her feelings to her friends, she's giving herself chance to process the change, so she may come to accept her new situation in time.

Option 6: This option is incorrect. Bruce is clearly expressing resistance when he calls the protocols "pointless." By expressing his negative feelings, he may be able to process them, but his assessment of what's happening in his company is not realistic and doesn't help him to move toward acceptance.

To help you gain a healthier perspective, you can express your feelings, use ceremony to mark the change, and assess your situation and its future prospects. Remember you can return to any of these strategies as needed to help you integrate and deal with your experience of change.

See each step in the process to find out more about it.

Express your feelings

It helps to have someone you can talk to, particularly when you're really battling with a difficult change. When choosing an appropriate listener, find someone you trust to listen empathetically, stay uninvolved, and keep confidentiality if need be.

If there is no-one you feel comfortable confiding in, you could also use a journal to write down and analyze what you're feeling.

Expressing your feelings helps you come to terms with your experiences, the reality of change, and the depth and range of your emotional responses. It allows you to voice your fears in a safe context, so you can explore, assess, and soothe them.

Use ceremony

People use ceremonies and rituals to mark the end of a phase in their lives and welcome the beginning of a new one.

You can create a ritual or ceremony for yourself, such as making a photograph album, or you can invite others to join your ceremony. Whatever ritual feels right for you can help you make your transition.

Organizations often use ceremonies such as farewell parties or staff induction programs for this very reason.

Assess your situation and future prospects

Think about your situation in a constructive way. First try to understand it better. Then assess possible outcomes and consequences. Focus on what you can gain from the change and how you can grow.

This helps you to gain a sense of control and come to grips with what's happening. It also helps you make the most of new opportunities.

Self-analysis

When you find yourself resisting organizational change, self-analysis can help you understand the source of your resistance and allow you to move forward into acceptance. Ask yourself questions to understand why you resist the change.

Useful questions for self-analysis

Hopefully your questions – and their answers – gave you insight into your resistance to change and helped you to become able to respond to it more constructively.

Questions that are generally useful for this process include - Why am I resisting change?
 - What is it in particular that triggers this reaction?
 - Who, if anyone, am I reacting to?
 - How am I acting out my feelings?
 - What is the issue exactly?
 - What constructive actions can I take about it?
 - What feelings can I set aside?

Several common emotional triggers drive resistance to change:
- feeling insecure,
- feeling inadequate or under-skilled,
- fearing failure for you and your organization,
- feelings of mistrust toward leaders and colleagues,
- worrying about personal problems that may interfere with your work life,
- feeling as if your position is being threatened, or
- having doubts about whether the decision to change is wise or whether strategies are well thought out.

Once you know your triggers or the source of your resistance, you can manage your feelings more constructively. As you become more self-aware, you master your emotional reactions and can investigate their causes.

For example, if you feel inadequate, you may become aware that it's specifically about your ability to perform a new role in your organization.

You can take action to remedy real gaps in your present capacity. For instance, you can ask for help or request additional training. You can also set your unfounded fears aside, because you understand them better. This boosts your confidence and makes it easier to move toward acceptance.

When Amrit's telecommunications company merges with a smaller competitor, she's asked to play a liaising role. However, she notices herself avoiding, and not approaching, her new colleagues. Follow along as she decides to get to the bottom of her feelings.

Organizational Change

I noticed I was feeling insecure and self-conscious whenever I had to approach someone from the other side of the merger.

I started asking myself, why am I feeling this way? What am I afraid of? I suddenly realized I assumed the newcomers were resentful of me and the merger. I was afraid they'd assume I'd treat them unfairly because they used to be our competition.

When I had to approach my new colleagues, I felt self-conscious for two reasons. First I was afraid they'd be hostile regardless of what I said or did. Second, I could easily cause further offense if I didn't handle this volatile issue sensitively.

These insights inspired me to suggest a series of small group workshops to enable new colleagues to bond and build trust. After all, I probably wasn't the only person feeling insecure.

Self-analysis actually helped me to fulfill my new role much more effectively. The merger became an exciting and satisfying process instead of something to fear.

Amrit uses self-analysis to move toward accepting change herself. In doing so, she identifies a real need in the organization and helps the merger to succeed. She's able to let go of her fears and be proactive.

Learning from the past

Even though change may feel unsettling now, you have weathered change in your past. Looking to past experiences reminds you you've survived change before and will do so in the future. If you feel anxious or resistant about change now, considering it in this context restores your balance.

Not only that, but you've already used strategies to adapt in earlier situations. So you can draw on your experience to empower you to make transitions in the present.

Consider what worked for you in the past and what didn't.

Eugene accepts a request from his retail company to help set up a new branch in another city, but is anxious he isn't going to make a success of it. Follow along as he reduces this anxiety by drawing on his past experiences.

I knew that I had to shape up or ship out. But thinking back to other major changes in my life was just getting me more anxious. So I decided to focus on a really small change.

I decided to revisit the time my company changed to a new operating system. At first, I tried to ignore the change as much as possible, but this didn't work. My colleagues became irritated with me and everything seemed to take twice as long.

Then I decided to read up on the new system and gave myself a few exercises to practice using it.

As I worked, I actually found out about a new feature that halved the time it took to collate my monthly reports. When I shared this with my supervisor, my new discovery became a formal step in the process.

So focusing on learning and practicing new ways of doing things has been useful to me in the past. It's also helpful to remember that I can be creative and initiate better ways of doing things – once I accept the challenge.

Remembering how I had coped with change in the past restored my balance, put things in context and boosted my confidence.

Eugene's able to plan for the change and to better accept it by reviewing a simple example from his past. He identifies what worked and what didn't then, and is now ready to apply his previous strategy for accepting change in his new situation.

Question

Which statements demonstrate that a person is moving from resistance to acceptance?

Options:

1. "I guess the change to online publication was inevitable."

2. "Part of the reason why I found it hard to work under a new management team was that I feared my previous achievements wouldn't be recognized."

3. "When I had to prove myself at work, I learned that it takes time. It's best to under-promise and over-deliver."

4. "This new situation will give me an opportunity to strengthen my skills and grow professionally."

5. "It doesn't make sense to do it differently now. In my experience it's completely unnecessary."

6. "I find it hard to work in a new team. This is chiefly because my colleagues' resist or are slow to accept new and innovative practices."

Answer:

Option 1: This option is correct. This statement demonstrates that the speaker gains perspective by recognizing change as inevitable. The speaker has accepted the change.

Option 2: This option is correct. By analyzing feelings and their origins, the speaker's demonstrating a move towards acceptance of change.

Option 3: This option is correct. By drawing on past experience, the speaker's becoming more confident and capable of adapting to a new situation.

Option 4: This option is correct. This statement demonstrates the speaker's assessing the present situation and future possibilities, which is a good way of gaining perspective.

Option 5: This option is incorrect. This statement demonstrates resistance to change, rather than a move toward acceptance, because it's not a constructive assessment.

Option 6: This option is incorrect. The statement expresses inflexibility, but shows no insight or self-analysis. Instead, the speaker is blaming external sources for these feelings.

Reframing attitudes toward change

It's often easy to identify the downside in change. But the problem with this type of attitude is that it doesn't help you face the future. Change won't go away, so you need to adopt a positive perspective to better come to terms with it.

Question

How positive is your attitude to change?

Options:

1. Very positive
2. Fairly positive
3. Not really positive

Answer:

Option 1: Congratulations. Your positive attitude helps you make the most of the situations you find yourself in and adapt to change effectively. This is because you're able to reframe potentially disruptive or negative change in a positive light.

Organizational Change

Option 2: You may notice that when your attitude is positive, you find it easier to make the most of your circumstances and adapt to change. You can use reframing to boost your positivity and become even more capable of responding effectively.

Option 3: Reframing could be a very useful tool for you. You can expect a more positive outlook to enhance your ability to make the most of the changing circumstances you find yourself in.

A creative strategy named "reframing" allows you to gain a more positive perspective on change. First you identify current beliefs and values around a particular issue – your frame of reference for dealing with a particular situation.

You then step back to notice the underlying attitude that colors your beliefs and values. You consciously adjust this attitude and adopt a different mindset with regards to the change.

Old patterns of response can keep you in a resistant state of mind. To move ahead in life, you sometimes need to learn new ways to think and respond to your environment.

Suppose you notice you're resisting change. Notice how you express your negative reaction in thought and words. Perhaps you're in a meeting and you realize you're thinking "This is a waste of my time." When you think this, you no longer listen and you stop contributing to the meeting.

When you reframe your thoughts to "What can I learn here and what can I offer?" your experience of the meeting changes to match these thoughts. Suddenly you find you have something to learn and to offer. The meeting no longer feels like a waste of time at all.

You can apply reframing in most situations where you find yourself thinking negative thoughts. "This is too difficult," becomes "Some of this is easy, and the difficult stuff is interesting." "I'm not experienced enough," becomes "I'm keen to learn." "My manager is being over-critical," becomes "My manager is helping me to achieve more."

Question

Consider some typical examples of negative statements and their possible reframes.

What are the good examples in which the negative attitude is correctly reframed?

Options:

1. "This new task is so boring." "I'll make this new task more interesting and fun."

2. "I'm not looking forward to working with new people." "Maybe my new colleagues will have a lot to offer."

3. "I always get the worst responsibilities." "I'm trusted to handle the most demanding work."

4. "I'll be laid off." "Maybe there's a new role for me in the company."

5. "I'm dreading this emergency meeting." "My contribution won't matter anyway."

6. "I'm never going to get this right." "It's not my fault my manager didn't think this through."

Answer:

Option 1: This option is correct. By reframing the new task as potentially interesting and fun, you make it more enjoyable and are more likely to do a good job.

Option 2: This option is correct. By replacing your negative expectations with positive ones, you help yourself to prepare for working with new people. So you feel more confident and have a better chance of success.

Option 3: This option is correct. When you consider your responsibilities as expressions of trust in your abilities, rather than favoritism, it's easier to have a positive attitude toward them.

Option 4: This option is correct. Reframing your fears into hopes gives you a more positive outlook, which boosts your confidence and your chances of making the most of new circumstances.

Option 5: This option is incorrect. By reframing your fearful thought into one of indifference, you reinforce your negative attitude, rather than replacing it with a positive one.

Option 6: This option is incorrect. By blaming management, you're not reframing the situation, you're simply shifting blame. Shifting the blame doesn't create a positive attitude.

Practical positives

Reframing works well for dealing with organizational change. You may never get to the point where you like the change, or would have chosen it yourself, but it can help you make peace with change. It can be an important step in the transition from passive acceptance to actively embracing change.

To reframe your thoughts about organizational change, search for its potential practical and emotional benefits.

See each type of benefit to find out more.

Practical benefits

Practical benefits are ways in which change might improve your professional situation in the short or long term. For example, if your company lays off employees, you may discover ways in which your career will benefit directly. It may give you work opportunities that wouldn't otherwise have been available.

If you have to learn new skills and processes, you may stand to gain specific skills or knowledge to advance your career. For example, perhaps you'll learn to use new software or receive more formal training.

Explore the specific ways in which these benefits may be valuable and how you can make the most of them.

Emotional benefits

Positive emotional outcomes are ways in which your emotional state improves as a result of change. A change at work may help you to feel happier, more contented, or more fulfilled.

Remember, new responsibilities or working with other colleagues can be exciting and fulfilling.

The future is uncertain so reframing isn't about identifying things that are bound to happen. It's about focusing on possible benefits you think change has a good chance of producing.

Consider the situation Loretta finds herself in. During the next few months, her marketing company is going to shift from an emphasis on working solo on projects to working in teams.

"At first I resented the idea. I'm good at what I do. Why do I need to change? But thinking this way made me feel worse, so I knew I had to change my attitude. To do this, I considered the possible benefits of the change. I'll spend less time on the computer, for one thing. Also, brainstorming is more effective if done in teams. So the initial conceptualization stages should be faster and better."

"Maybe teamwork will enhance creativity. It'll definitely be easier to pull things together. I might not have to spend hours or days waiting for people to get back to me, like I do now. The many potential advantages of the change are making me look forward to teamwork."

Now consider Jason. He works for a footwear factory who recently automated processes that were previously done manually. When he first heard about the change, he worried about being laid off and not being able to pay off his home loan.

"But as it turned out, I was trained on the new machinery instead of losing my job. Not only that, but I have a strong feeling that my manager wants me to learn how to service it."

"I'm more secure in my job than ever before and I have a chance to develop my skills as the industry develops. I think there may even be a raise in the near future."

Question

Both Loretta and Jason had initial misgivings about change in their organizations.

Which comments did they make that show how they reframed their situations by finding practical benefits?

Options:

1. "The many potential advantages of the change are making me look forward to teamwork."

2. "Maybe teamwork will enhance creativity."

3. "...I have a chance to develop my skills as the industry develops."

4. "...there may even be a raise in the near future."

5. "I'm good at what I do."

6. "Why do I need to change?"

Answer:

Option 1: This option is correct. Recognizing she has something to look forward to shows that Loretta is reframing her outlook. She's considering the positive practical benefits that change can bring.

Organizational Change

Option 2: This option is correct. Loretta is looking for potential benefits to her company's new emphasis on teamwork, which demonstrates she's reframing her outlook.

Option 3: This option is correct. Jason recognizes the potential positive outcomes of the automation of his factory's manufacturing process. This shows he's reframing his situation.

Option 4: This option is correct. Jason is hopeful the changes in his organization may lead to a raise. This demonstrates he's reframing his outlook, which increases his motivation to accept the changes.

Option 5: This option is incorrect. When Loretta says she's good at her job, she's actually expressing her resistance to change, not reframing her situation.

Option 6: This option is incorrect. Loretta's imagining possible negative outcomes. She isn't reframing because she's dwelling on the way she did her job in the past.

Emotional positives

Searching for emotionally positive benefits is an important way of reframing your situation. This helps you make peace with organizational change and perhaps even become enthusiastic about what it has to offer.

Think about current duties or colleagues who have a negative emotional impact on you. Then consider potential changes that might have a positive emotional impact and enable you to do more.

Negative colleagues – natural pessimists or those who are unsupportive of you – can have a negative effect on your emotional state. So too can tasks that you find unstimulating or overfamiliar. You reframe your emotions about these colleagues or tasks when you focus on the positive emotional benefit which comes from escaping such negative influences.

You know which work you find particularly enjoyable or stimulating. Perhaps you are, or could be, really good at it. Change may allow you to spend more time on it, so work becomes more pleasurable.

Sara's being moved from her job in the warehouse to the research team preparing regular sales reports for senior management. Follow along as she goes through a reframing exercise to look at this change in a positive light.

I felt so nervous about working on the research team. What if I don't meet their standards? Everybody at the head office seems so competent and well-qualified.

So, to become more confident, I decided to reframe the situation and I focused on the positive emotional benefits of the change. Surely, they wouldn't have offered me the position if I didn't have the potential to do it.

First I thought about what made me unhappy at the warehouse. I noticed the work there had become routine and I was bored. I find working to deadlines as part of the research team stimulating. Getting new challenges at work will be a welcome relief.

Then I asked myself what would make me happy in the new role. I really like knowing about the bigger picture, so preparing sales reports should be very interesting. I'm sure I'll be good at it. There's so much to learn – I hope I'm up to it.

Sara reframes her situation by identifying the emotional benefits of her move to the research team. She identifies negative emotional triggers in her situation at the warehouse and focuses on how the new situation allows her to escape these. However, she doesn't reframe as effectively as she could have done, so she may still feel more apprehensive than she needs to be about the move.

Question

Which of Sara's statements demonstrate that she reframed her situation?

Options:

1. "Surely, they wouldn't have offered me the position if I didn't have the potential to do it."
2. "Getting new challenges at work will be a welcome relief."
3. "...I focused on the positive emotional benefits of the change."
4. "...I asked myself what would make me happy in the new role."
5. "There's so much to learn – I hope I'm up to it."
6. "Everybody at head office seems so competent and well-qualified."

Answer:

Option 1: This option is correct. Sara initially felt nervous and that she might not be up to her new responsibilities. So reassuring herself that her managers feel she's capable is a good way for her to reframe her situation.

Option 2: This option is correct. Sara's reframing her situation by searching for ways in which the change will free her from negative emotional triggers she experienced in her pervious situation.

Option 3: This option is correct. By thinking about new opportunities to do work that make her happy, Sara's reframing her situation very effectively.

Option 4: This option is correct. Sara's reframing her situation when she thinks about being freed from negative emotional triggers when working in the warehouse.

Option 5: This option is incorrect. This statement didn't reframe Sara's anxiety about being capable of doing well in her new position. Instead, it reinforces her feeling of inadequacy.

Option 6: This option is incorrect. This statement makes Sara feel more nervous, because she's comparing herself unfavorably with her capable future colleagues. So it doesn't demonstrate reframing.

Capitalizing on change

Organizational change can be tough, but why not take the lemons you've been given and make lemonade? By being proactive and reframing change, you'll find yourself seizing fresh opportunities and capitalizing on them, thereby increasing your motivation, empowering yourself, feeling inspired, and advancing your career.

Question

Do you make lemonade from lemons? How proactive have you been about capitalizing on organizational change?

Options:

1. Very
2. Somewhat
3. Not at all

Answer:

Option 1: By proactively seizing fresh opportunities, you've most probably realized the benefits of capitalizing on organizational change and, besides having seen your career advance, you're probably feeling inspired, empowered, and motivated.

Option 2: When you become more proactive, internalize reframing, and capitalize on the opportunities presented by organizational change, you'll be even better able to advance your career, feel more motivated and inspired, and become fully self-empowered.

Option 3: You'll be able to capitalize on organizational change only when you proactively reframe it and seize the fresh opportunities it offers you. When you do this, you'll find that your career will advance, you'll feel more motivated and inspired, and you'll experience the benefits of your own empowerment.

People who feel victimized by fate end up drifting on the currents of change. But this doesn't have to be true of you. You can set your own course and actively pursue your goals. When you're proactive about organizational change, you regain a sense of control and can get the passion back into your work life.

See each benefit of capitalizing on organizational change to find out more about it.

Regain a sense of control

Being proactive puts you in the driver's seat of your professional life. By defining your new role in the change process, you gain a real say in what you do at work. Taking initiative helps you feel more in control and decisive action helps you regain some control in your working life.

For example, you could volunteer your translation skills when your company expands to a foreign country to secure a future role in the expansion.

You can also approach your colleagues with ideas, questions, and possibilities instead of simply going along with whatever arises.

Get the passion back

If your work life has lost its sense of fun and excitement, you can get the passion back by proactively capitalizing on organizational change.

To do this, explore the activities that bring you stimulation, inspiration, and pleasure. Notice what you enjoy doing now. Then actively use the new opportunities to steer your career toward these activities.

If you notice that relating to people is the highlight of your day, for instance, negotiate a change of role so you interact with people more.

Question

What are the benefits of proactively capitalizing on organizational change?

Options:

1. You'll feel more in control
2. You'll be able to get the passion back in your working life
3. You'll be able to earn more
4. You'll be able to boost your productivity

Answer:

Option 1: This option is correct. The more proactive you are about capitalizing on organizational change, the more you'll feel a sense of control over your working life.

Option 2: This option is correct. If your working life lacks passion, you can get it back by proactively capitalizing on organizational change.

Option 3: This option is incorrect. While capitalizing on change can result in promotion and increased income,

Organizational Change

you can't be assured this will happen. The main advantage of capitalizing on change is that it alters the way you feel about your work.

Option 4: This option is incorrect. Proactively capitalizing on some types of organizational change may boost productivity in specific instances, but it's not a given.

Reinventing yourself

Once you've used reframing to shift your response, you can move on to the second step in capitalizing on change. So how do you use opportunities to reap the benefits of organizational change? You need to reinvent yourself.

Reinventing yourself means expanding your ideas of who you are and redefining what you're capable of achieving. For example, if you're knowledgeable in several key areas and are a good decision-maker, but have never considered yourself a potential manager, perhaps it's time to redefine your abilities.

Many of the skills you possess can be used in different contexts or roles. For example, you could put your experience of negotiation and financial records gained in HR to good use in acquisitions, sales, or marketing.

If you don't reinvent yourself, you're likely to stagnate at a lower level of responsibility than you're capable of. If you have a narrow definition of what you can do, others buy into it. Open yourself to change, growth, and opportunity, and you show others you're ready for a new challenge.

To reinvent yourself, you need to disengage from your old professional identity and from your routines and established ways of doing things. So disengagement is about letting go of your old organizational role and self-definitions at work and focusing on your new role.

Disengagement gives you the necessary distance from the way you worked in the past, so you can move forward. However, it's not simply about setting everything aside indiscriminately.

Rather, you need to assess yourself, review your past experiences, and consciously decide what aspects of your role and identity you want to keep and what to discard. You can then integrate old and new qualities to function better in your new context.

To reinvent yourself, ask the following questions:

What aspects of my professional identity, ways of doing things, and routines should I disengage from when my role changes?

- What should I choose to keep?
- What new possibilities inspire me?
- What new capabilities will help me succeed and how can I develop them?
- How do I integrate old and new definitions of myself and my capabilities?
- How do I integrate old and new?

Bruce occupies a low-profile position in his company's Information Technology department. As a hobby, he dabbles in mathematical statistics. When his organization wins a bid to computerize the city's commuter transit services, he wants to be a part of the change. Follow along as Bruce reinvents himself.

Computerizing the city's transit services sounds fascinating – I know I could thrive in this role. But before I can capitalize on this new opportunity, I know I have to reinvent myself and trust that I can really do this.

I need to let go of my comfortable under-the-radar approach to work. I'm capable of more. What do I need to disengage from?

My efficiency and familiarity with programming will be an asset for this new opportunity.

I need to take ownership of my expertise in statistical analysis and I need to develop my understanding of the mathematical theories so I can apply it to a system design that would really work.

I think I'm ready to rise to the challenge!

Question

Maria is the production manager for a software components company. Her company has decided to implement major changes to its product line. Maria knows she needs to reinvent herself to make the most of this new opportunity.

Which actions are examples of her doing this?

Options:

1. Reviewing her past experience in setting up new production lines

2. Asking herself how she can build on her capabilities with the new production-line equipment

3. Asking herself what old production routines she can disengage from

4. Asking herself what new roles she can take on

5. Reducing her commitments to supply-chain management

6. Discussing new opportunities with her colleagues

Answer:

Option 1: This option is correct. Reviewing your past experiences enables Maria to assess what she can disengage from and what she can bring into play in a new context.

Option 2: This option is correct. Reinventing herself requires Maria to develop new capabilities.

Option 3: This option is correct. Maria disengages from old routines to reinvent herself.

Option 4: This option is correct. By seeking new roles for herself in the organization, Maria's redefining and therefore reinventing herself.

Option 5: This option is incorrect. Reinventing herself doesn't require Maria to reduce her present commitments.

Option 6: This option is incorrect. While discussing new opportunities with colleagues is helpful, it's not part of reinventing herself.

Realigning career goals

Organizational change can be a unique opportunity to change your career or advance it. Advancing your career is the third step in capitalizing on change. Using this step, you can expand your horizons, grow, and learn. But to bring these possibilities into your life, you need to reevaluate and realign your career goals.

By capitalizing on change, you actively seek success and passion, and feel like you're in control. Instead of simply surviving the change, you can reach your full potential.

Having a vision of your future career and dreaming of what you could achieve allows you to reap the potential benefits of change.

Just imagining what the future can hold is not enough. Clear goals, objectives, and strategies are essential to changing dreams into reality.

Your former job may have been very well aligned with your strengths, values, and priorities. But the post-change reality may no longer be such a comfortable fit. If this is

Organizational Change

the case, organizational change may force you to revise your career.

Have you ever changed your career? What kinds of problems arose for you when your career changed?

When your career changes, your daily activities change, which is disruptive. Your priorities, values, and sources of fulfillment at work could be thrown into question. Each of these may need to be redefined, modified, or reassessed. If your career isn't integrated with the changes you experience, you may feel out of control and unhappy.

So to integrate and express your personal priorities, values, and sources of fulfillment, you need to examine them and ask yourself how – and if – you would like to amend them.

Angela's game lodge has merged with a corporate hotel chain. Before the merger, the lodge was scrupulous about preserving the natural habitat of the area's fauna and flora. Follow along as Angela considers her new role as communications manager for the chain.

This change has been so difficult and I'm really feeling helpless. But I know I need to think outside the box on the issue of the development that management is likely to introduce.

Whereas the lodge promoted our natural habitat, I'm worried that the chain will put profit before ecological preservation. I really don't feel comfortable about promoting this.

I am capable of doing a good job – there are all sorts of mitigating factors. But when I listen to my heart, I also know that I won't feel proud of myself or fulfilled in my work if I take this on.

I'd better make an appointment with my manager to discuss my position and figure out how we can work around it.

As Angela's situation demonstrates, when organizational change impacts on your career, you need to ask yourself whether your personal needs and career goals can align with your new reality. You also need to ask yourself if the change has opened up new positions you should apply for.

See each self-assessment area to find out more about it.

Do my personal needs and career goals align with the new reality?

Before you synchronize your career with organizational change, you first need to investigate your personal needs and career goals. Then you can decide if it's possible – or desirable – to go ahead.

Investigate how well these goals and needs match the opportunities the organizational change presents.

For instance, if your organization is putting new emphasis on corporate responsibility, and you're strongly motivated by a desire to benefit others, this would be a good fit.

Has the change opened up new positions?

Proactively investigate whether new positions have been created or old ones modified in ways that are compatible with your goals and passions.

For example, if your organization creates a new management position, you may be well placed to play the leadership role that comes naturally to you.

Question

Tom is the head landscaper for a local chain of hotels that's recently changed ownership. He prides himself on his attention to native plantings and his eco-friendly gardening methods. The new owners want to upscale their image and expand into other regions. They envision the landscaping architecture to prominently figure into the newer upscale "brand." They need a landscape architect to lead the project and oversee the team making the change. Though his current job is mostly "hands on" working in the gardens, Tom does have a degree in Landscape Architecture.

What sorts of things could Tom do or ask himself to realign his career goals?

Options:

1. Think about what kind of landscaping he feels passionate about

2. Check that he can still work flexible hours to look after his special-needs child

3. Investigate whether he could move into a supervisory position

4. Think about what his ideal job would be like

5. Prepare to leave his organization

6. Prepare to sacrifice his indigenous gardening principles to take on a more commercial approach

Answer:

Option 1: This option is correct. To realign his career goals, Tom first needs to assess his values, priorities, and passions.

Option 2: This option is correct. When Tom is realigning his career goals, he needs to check that his personal needs can still be met when his organization changes.

Option 3: This option is correct. Investigating the possibility of a new position helps Tom realign his career goals with changes in his organization.

Option 4: This option is correct. Thinking about what his ideal job would be like helps Tom define his career goals, so he can align them with changes.

Option 5: This option is incorrect. Even if change doesn't go the way Tom hopes, it's possible for him to modify his role in the chain of hotels.

Option 6: This option is incorrect. Sacrificing his principles won't help Tom realign his career goals. Instead, he should try to match his principles with the practical situation and possibilities in his organization.

Creating career plans

Once you've identified your career goals, you need to create a flexible career plan that you can review and redraft, as necessary.

A career plan allows you to explore your professional ambitions, your strategies to achieve them, and what actions you need to take. It fleshes out the details and organizes your thoughts.

As your role in your organization changes, your career plan helps you to contextualize the transition in terms of your career goals. This places a more positive spin on your transition experience.

Although each career plan is unique, the structure should always include the following elements – an ideal work description, long and short term goal statements, personal needs and circumstances, and an action plan.

See each career-plan element to find out more about it.

1. Ideal work description

Think about what your ideal job would be like. Who would you work with? What benefits do you want your work to produce for yourself and others? How would you like to work? And how much would you like to earn in the future?

When you have a description of your ideal work or job, you can use it as a benchmark for your career plans.

2. Long and short-term goal statements

Making statements about your goals helps to make your vision of your career more concrete. Your goals should be specific, feasible, structured, and focused on getting results.

Long-term goals are goals you want to achieve in the next three to five years. They give you something to strive toward.

Short-term goals can be projected over the next year to year and a half. They clarify what you're working toward and how you should proceed.

3. Personal needs and circumstances

Your personal needs and circumstances affect the feasibility of your career goals. Additionally, without the balance of your personal life, you and your career are at risk.

This section of your career plan should include the personal resources you need to draw on to be successful, such as savings, equipment, contacts, and support systems.

It should also include realistic limits that your personal commitments and resources place on what you can achieve. For instance, if you have a family to raise or a long daily commute, you have less time to invest.

4. Action plan

Organizational Change

Once you've carefully considered the first three elements, you can create an action plan.

You use your action plan to set schedules and procedures around short-term goals. Your action plan should be pragmatic and contain realistic milestones. This keeps you on track and gives you a way of monitoring your progress. Set evaluation dates in your action plan so you can assess your progress.

Don't give yourself a plan that's too demanding. If circumstances change, be ready to modify it accordingly.

Once you realign your career goals to your new reality, you can better target opportunities change creates for you. For example, if a department in your company is restructured, you could target a management position that's a good fit for your long-term career goals.

Question

Match each description to the career plan element that it describes.

Options:

A. The work you would find most fulfilling
B. Brief statements of what you want to achieve
C. Factors at home
D. A chronological to-do list

Targets:

1. Ideal work description
2. Long- and short-term goal statements 3. Personal needs and circumstances
4. Action plan

Answer:

Your ideal work description is where you explore what work you enjoy most

Brief expressions of what you want to achieve are long- and short-term goals statements.

Factors at home that limit or enhance your goals are personal needs and circumstances.

A chronological to-do list is an action plan.

www.ingramcontent.com/pod-product-compliance
Lightning Source LLC
Chambersburg PA
CBHW020920180526
45163CB00007B/2816